"To be a slave. To be owned by another person, as a car, house or table is owned. To live as a piece of property that could be sold—a child sold from its mother, a wife from her husband. To be considered not human, but a thing that plowed the fields, cut the wood, cooked the food, nursed another's child; a thing whose sole function was determined by the one who owned you.

"To be a slave. To know despite the suffering and deprivation, that you were human, more human than he who said you were not human. To know joy, laughter, sorrow, and tears and yet be considered only the equal of a table. To be a slave was to be a human being under conditions in which that humanity was denied. They were not slaves. They were people. Their condition was slavery."

—Julius Lester

SLAVERY
THE STRUGGLE FOR FREEDOM

By James Meadows

COVER PHOTO

Three Abyssinian slaves in chains
© Bettmann/Corbis

Published in the United States of America by The Child's World®, Inc.
PO Box 326
Chanhassen, MN 55317-0326
800-599-READ
www.childsworld.com

Product Manager Mary Francis-DeMarois/The Creative Spark
Designer Robert E. Bonaker/Graphic Design & Consulting Co.
Editorial Direction Elizabeth Sirimarco Budd
Contributors Mary Berendes, Red Line Editorial, Katherine Stevenson, Ph.D.

The Child's World®, Inc., and Journey to Freedom® are the sole property
and registered trademarks of The Child's World®, Inc.

Library of Congress Cataloging-in-Publication Data
Meadows, James, 1969–
Slavery : the struggle for freedom / by James Meadows.
p. cm.
Includes bibliographical references and index.
ISBN 1-56766-923-9 (lib. bdg. : alk. paper)
1. Slavery—United States—History—Juvenile literature.
2. Slavery—America—History—Juvenile literature. 3. Slaves—United
States—Social conditions—Juvenile literature. 4. Slaves—America—Social
conditions—Juvenile literature. 5. African Americans—History—To 1863—Juvenile literature.
6. Blacks—America—History—Juvenile literature. [1. Slavery—History.]
I. Title.
E441 .M48 2001
973'.0496—dc21
2001002234

Contents

The Beginning   6

Slavery in North America   14

A Slave's Life   20

Resistance   26

Slavery's End   30

Timeline   36

Glossary   37

Index   39

Further Information   40

The Beginning

The first slave ships set sail from Europe around 1450, more than 500 years ago. They sailed to Africa from the country of Portugal. At the time, Portugal was one of the wealthiest, most powerful nations in Europe. Even so, it did not have enough farm workers. Portuguese slave traders captured Africans and brought them back to Europe.

Soon, other Europeans, as well as Arab slave traders from North Africa, became active in the slave trade. They took people from central Africa to sell not only in Europe, but in Eastern lands such as Arabia and India. Later, beginning in 1619, slave traders shipped Africans across the Atlantic Ocean to the "New World." Once there, the **enslaved** Africans were sold like livestock. They were forced to work on farms, clean houses, or anything else their masters wanted. They worked long hours for no pay. If they refused to work, they were often beaten or sometimes killed.

European slave traders made a huge **profit** by selling human beings into **bondage.** The slave ships sailed south from Europe toward West Africa, where African women, men, and children were going about their lives. Some were blacksmiths and miners. Others were farmers, priests, and politicians. They were leaders and warriors, parents and children. Millions of African people were torn from their families, their homes, their land, and their gods. They were chained and packed into ships like sacks of grain. The voyage across the Atlantic Ocean took months. Up to one in three of the Africans died of hunger, disease, and despair along the way.

Slavery ended almost 150 years ago, but learning about it today helps us understand the **racism** and **prejudice** that still exist. We can be inspired by the courage of those who endured slavery and those who fought to end it. And we can better appreciate our nation's struggle to hold true to its values of freedom and equality.

North Wind Pictures

EUROPEAN SLAVE TRADERS FIRST CAPTURED AFRICANS TO SELL IN
AMERICA IN THE EARLY 1600s. SLAVERY HAD EXISTED IN OTHER
PARTS OF THE WORLD THROUGHOUT HISTORY.

Africa is the second largest continent on Earth. It stretches almost 5,000 miles from the Mediterranean Sea in the north to the Cape of Good Hope in the south. Within that great land lie two of the world's largest deserts (the Sahara and the Kalahari), endless plains, and miles of rain forest. The Nile River, the longest river on Earth, also flows through Africa.

Africa's people are as **diverse** as their land. Africans live everywhere on the continent and speak hundreds of different languages. Before slavery, Africans lived in giant empires and small villages. Tribes and **clans** often had very different religious traditions and customs. When slave traders first arrived, Africans had a hard time banding together to fight back because their languages and customs were often so different. Many Africans who were captured and taken to slave ships felt completely alone, even when surrounded by other Africans.

Slavery existed in Africa even before Europeans came. Africans sometimes kept other Africans as slaves. The African version of slavery was somewhat different from the slavery that came later. When African clans were at war, captured soldiers often became slaves. These captives sometimes became part of their new culture rather than staying slaves all their lives. They often married into the new clan. Sometimes slaves rose to positions of leadership and power.

When European slave traders captured Africans and sent them to other countries, the result was different. Almost all these enslaved Africans remained slaves their entire lives. Their children were born into slavery as well. The slaves were not accepted into the world of their white masters. They could not rise to positions of power. Soon after slavery reached North America, lawmakers even made it illegal for slaves to learn to read. And although many enslaved Africans had lifelong partners and families, they could not legally marry.

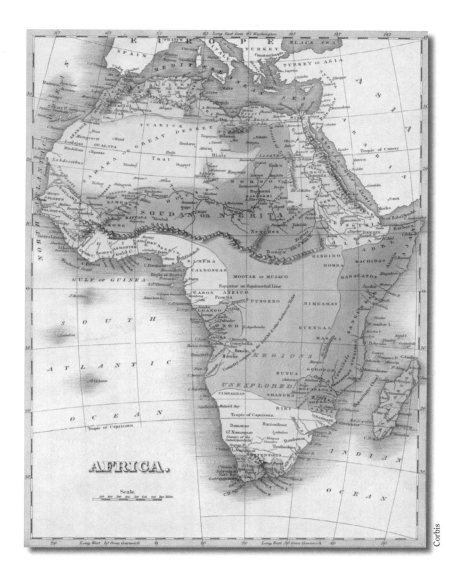

AFRICA IS A HUGE CONTINENT, AS THIS 19TH-CENTURY MAP SHOWS. DIVERSE PEOPLE LIVE ACROSS THE LAND AND SPEAK HUNDREDS OF DIFFERENT LANGUAGES. FOR THIS REASON, MANY AFRICANS FELT COMPLETELY ALONE AS THEY WERE FORCED ONTO SLAVE SHIPS AND TRANSPORTED TO AMERICA.

When European slave traders came to Africa to capture new slaves, they did not work alone. Other Africans often helped them. Why did they do this? Different African clans often had little in common. Just as Europeans from different countries often fought each other, Africans were sometimes bitter enemies of other Africans. Europeans also bribed Africans with cloth, guns, and other forms of wealth. Africans who cooperated with the Europeans received guns that could help them defeat their enemies. Later, Africans helped Europeans capture other Africans to avoid being sold into slavery themselves.

During the time of slavery, most Europeans believed that Africans were savage and stupid. They believed that Africans were not quite human and needed whites to guide them. That was how Europeans justified slavery. History tells a different story about African cultures. Many Africans lived in large, wealthy kingdoms such as Ghana, Mali, and Songhay. Ghana was the oldest of the three kingdoms.

Songhay eventually became the wealthiest. It was as great as any empire in the world at that time.

So what happened to these great African empires? The slave trade changed the entire region. Every year, European slave traders and their African helpers captured thousands of the empires' strongest, most capable people. The captives were shipped to the other side of the world, year after year, for hundreds of years. Many people believe the slave trade set African societies back hundreds of years.

Why did Europeans create such a brutal trade? The answer requires a little background. In the 1490s and early 1500s, European explorers sailed across the Atlantic looking for a faster, cheaper way to the Asian lands of India and China. The Europeans wanted to go to Asia to buy silks, spices, and other exotic goods Europe lacked. But instead of finding better routes to India and China, the explorers accidentally found the continents we now call North and South America.

Corbis

SADLY, EUROPEANS WERE NOT THE ONLY PEOPLE INVOLVED IN THE SLAVE TRADE. SOMETIMES AFRICANS SOLD PEOPLE FROM OTHER TRIBES INTO SLAVERY.

Europeans decided to claim the vast lands of this "New World." But although this world was new to the Europeans, it was already home to millions of Native Americans. As the Europeans took the land from the Native Americans, they needed more people to grow crops, build towns, and provide goods and services. They wanted this work done as cheaply as possible so they could keep more money for themselves.

First the Europeans tried enslaving Native Americans, but without success. Many of the Native Americans were hunters more than farmers and were not well suited to the work the Europeans forced them to do. A vast number died from diseases the Europeans brought with them. Still more died from **inhumane** treatment. Also, the Native Americans knew the land well enough to escape. And they could sometimes fight back, because their own people lived nearby.

When enslaving Native Americans proved unsuccessful, the Europeans brought in African slaves instead. Many of the new slaves had been farmers in Africa and were used to the work. They had already been exposed to many of the diseases the Europeans brought from the Old World. And they were less likely to escape, because they did not know this strange land and had nowhere to go. The only people who could help them were back in Africa, thousands of miles away.

The European slave traders shipped millions of Africans to places throughout the New World. No one knows the exact number. Some people estimate 9 million, and others estimate up to 25 million. Most of the Africans were shipped to Caribbean Islands such as Hispaniola (present-day Haiti and the Dominican Republic), Jamaica, Puerto Rico, and Cuba. The next largest group went to South and Central America. A smaller number were transported to North America.

North Wind Pictures

THE FIRST SLAVES TO ARRIVE IN AMERICA
LANDED IN JAMESTOWN, PART OF THE
COLONY OF VIRGINIA. SLAVERY SPREAD
QUICKLY THROUGHOUT THE COLONIES,
ESPECIALLY IN FARMING AREAS.

Slavery in North America

The voyage across the Atlantic Ocean to North America, often called the "Middle Passage," was long and cruel. Africans captured inland in Africa were sometimes forced to march hundreds of miles to the coast. During this exhausting journey, they were tied at the hands and neck. They marched all day and far into the evening, stopping only for a little food and water. Those who could not keep up were beaten or left to die. Once the captives reached the coast, they were loaded onto slave ships.

The more slaves each ship carried, the more money the slave traders made. The traders packed as many slaves as they could onto the ships that crossed the Atlantic. The captives were chained to the deck for days at a time. They were packed in shoulder to shoulder and hip to hip. Usually they had too little headroom to sit up. Forced to lie in their own waste and vomit, they fell victim to deadly diseases such as smallpox. Conditions aboard the overcrowded ships were so awful that one third of the captives never survived the trip. Some even killed themselves, jumping overboard to escape the misery.

The first enslaved Africans landed in North America in 1619. Many whites who traveled to the New World at this time dreamed of earning great wealth or enjoying religious freedom. The first Africans had no such opportunities waiting for them. Instead, they landed in chains, half a world away from their families and their communities. They did not know the land or the language of their captors. They had no way to return home. These first Africans were enslaved—but not for life. Instead, if they worked for 7 to 10 years, they were set free.

THE VOYAGE SLAVES TOOK ACROSS THE ATLANTIC OCEAN IS OFTEN CALLED
THE MIDDLE PASSAGE—THE MIDDLE OR SECOND LEG OF THEIR JOURNEY TO
A LIFE OF SLAVERY. DURING THE EARLIER FIRST LEG, THE CAPTIVES WERE
MARCHED IN CHAINS TO THE AFRICAN COASTS AND THE WAITING SLAVE SHIPS.
THE FINAL LEG OF THE JOURNEY WAS IN AMERICA, WHERE THE SLAVES WERE
TRANSPORTED TO BE SOLD AT AUCTION.

These freed slaves and their families were among the "free blacks" living in North America during later years of slavery. But the opportunity for earning freedom did not last long. Soon wealthy landowners saw that they could make more money by keeping the Africans enslaved for life. New laws made it more difficult to free blacks and increased the punishment for slaves who ran away. By law, the children of slaves also became slaves. By 1650, slavery in North America meant a life of bondage passed from one generation to the next.

Many people believe that slavery existed only in the South, but that is not true. Before the United States won its independence from England, slavery existed in every single American colony. Enslaved blacks worked in shops in the North and on **plantations** in the South. Slavery continued even after founding father Thomas Jefferson wrote in the Declaration of Independence that "all men are created equal." In fact, Jefferson himself owned slaves! So did George Washington. Both men had mixed feelings about slavery but continued to own slaves.

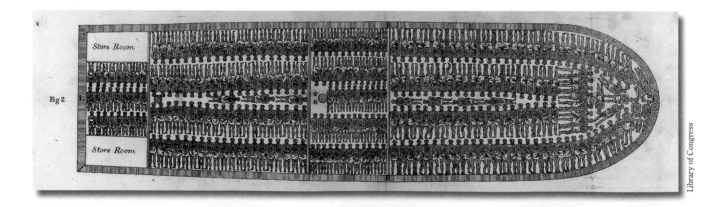

Store Room

Fig 2.

Store Room

THE IMAGE ABOVE SHOWS A PLAN FOR A SHIP'S SLAVE QUARTERS. AFRICANS WERE TRANSPORTED TO SLAVERY UNDER TERRIBLE CONDITIONS. THEY WERE CROWDED ONTO SHIPS AND FORCED UNDER THE DECK INTO DARK, DIRTY, SLAVE QUARTERS. OVER THE YEARS, AN ESTIMATED 1.8 MILLION SLAVES DIED DURING THE VOYAGE ACROSS THE ATLANTIC.

Library of Congress

THE UNITED STATES WAS FOUNDED ON THE IDEA OF FREEDOM, BUT MANY OF THE FOUNDING FATHERS, INCLUDING GEORGE WASHINGTON AND THOMAS JEFFERSON, OWNED SLAVES. WASHINGTON IS SHOWN HERE (SECOND FROM RIGHT) WITH SEVERAL SLAVES AT MOUNT VERNON, HIS VIRGINIA PLANTATION.

MANY PEOPLE THINK OF SLAVERY AS HAVING EXISTED ONLY IN THE SOUTH, BUT FOR MANY YEARS PEOPLE IN THE NORTH HAD SLAVES, TOO. HERE A SLAVE IN THE COLONY OF NEW YORK WELCOMES HOME HIS MASTER.

After the United States won its independence from England, the states in the North **abolished** slavery, one by one. People there reasoned that if they truly believed in freedom, they could not allow slavery to exist in their states. Many people also saw that slave labor, especially in the cities, was not much cheaper than hiring workers. People in the South had a different view. They refused to give up slavery. The disagreement between the North and the South almost split the new nation in two. Northerners avoided a break by allowing slavery into the **Constitution.** More than 70 years later, the same disagreement would help spark this nation's **Civil War.**

Abolishing slavery in the North created large populations of free blacks in those states. Free blacks did not have the same rights as whites, but they had more rights than enslaved blacks. Many free blacks in the North used their freedom to help slaves escape.

North Wind Pictures

By the middle of the 18th century, 90 percent of all slaves in America lived in the South. This was because the Southern states were filled with plantations that depended on the free labor the slaves provided.

A Slave's Life

For many blacks, life in the New World began on the auction block. The auction block was a place, often in the center of town, where cows, horses, and slaves were bought and sold. Most slave owners were looking for slaves who were strong. Strong slaves could work long and hard, plowing the land and picking crops such as corn, tobacco, and cotton. The buyers poked and prodded the new arrivals. They checked their teeth as if the slaves were horses. They read posters that advertised both livestock and slaves. The black captives stood naked and chained while the white farmers inspected them. To many of the white farmers, the enslaved blacks were not human. They were little more than animals bought to perform certain tasks.

It is not easy to make someone work long hours for no pay. White slave owners used cruelty to force the slaves to work. Slaves could be whipped for not working fast enough, for not getting out to the fields by dawn, or for almost anything else. They could be whipped by the master, the master's wife or children, or the **overseer.** Masters of larger farms often hired an overseer to make sure the slaves worked hard, did not rebel, and did not run away. Many overseers were known for being exceptionally cruel.

Frederick Douglass, an **abolitionist** and **fugitive** slave, described his overseer: "Mr. Severe was rightly named; he was a cruel man. I have seen him whip a woman, causing the blood to run half an hour at a time; and this too, in the midst of her crying children pleading for their mother's release."

The whips used for punishment were often several feet long and made of stiff cowhide. A single stroke of the whip could draw blood. Several strokes could make a person unconscious from the pain or even kill someone.

North Wind Pictures

AFTER SLAVES ARRIVED IN AMERICA, THEY WERE SOLD AT AUCTION, JUST LIKE LIVESTOCK OR SUPPLIES.

Slave owners often separated families by selling children away from their parents. Husbands could be sold away from their wives, and brothers and sisters could be separated from one another. These separations were common. Frederick Douglass wrote, "I never saw my mother, to know her as such, more than four or five times in my life.... She died when I was about seven years old, on one of my master's farms, near Lee's Mill. I was not allowed to be present during her illness, at her death, or burial. She was gone long before I knew anything about it."

It was illegal to teach a slave to read. Slave owners sometimes disobeyed this law, but most enslaved blacks were not given the chance to learn. Most were not allowed to know anything about their personal history. Frederick Douglass wrote, "By far the larger part of the slaves know as little of their ages as horses know of theirs, and it is the wish of most masters within my knowledge to keep their slaves thus ignorant."

Why would slave owners break up families? And why would they keep slaves from learning to read, or even knowing how old they were? They did it to keep the slaves completely **dependent** on their masters. How far could an escaped slave run without knowing how to read? Enslaved children without parents were dependent on their white masters no matter how cruel they were. Dependent slaves were less likely to run away or kill their masters.

Even today, a few people say that slavery was not so bad. After all, they argue, slaves were housed and fed, and all they had to do was put in an honest day's work. In truth, slaves rarely were given enough to eat—perhaps a pint of rice or grain and less than a pound of meat for a whole week. Many of us could easily eat that amount of food in one day! Often the food was rotten. As for shelter, slave quarters looked more like horse barns than houses. The rough boards did not keep the wind out or the heat in. There were no beds.

North Wind Pictures

AMONG THE GREATEST TRAGEDIES OF SLAVERY WAS
THE FACT THAT FAMILIES WERE OFTEN SEPARATED
FROM EACH OTHER. CHILDREN AND SPOUSES COULD
BE SOLD AT ANY TIME, NEVER TO BE SEEN AGAIN.

SLAVES LIVED IN COLD, DARK CABINS, OFTEN SHARING CRAMPED, ONE-ROOM QUARTERS WITH SEVERAL OTHER PEOPLE.

Instead, the slaves slept on narrow boards or a dirt floor. Nothing in the slaves' lives belonged to them— not their clothes, their homes, their children, their work, or even their bodies. Slave owners regularly took advantage of their female "property." They had complete freedom to do so because no laws protected female slaves against rape.

Even off the plantation, enslaved blacks had very little freedom. They were not allowed to leave the plantation without permission from the master. They could not meet in groups even to talk about the weather. They could not buy or sell goods or hire themselves out to do a job. They were not allowed to have guns. They could not even beat drums. Almost any white person could whip or beat an enslaved black. Slaves had no legal protection from any white person on or off the master's farm. Slave owners might call the law if someone threatened their slave "property," but no slave could seek any protection from the law, no matter what happened.

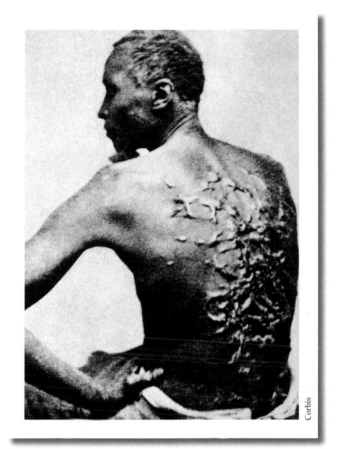

Corbis

Many white lawmakers knew the terrible conditions under which slaves were brought across the Atlantic. In 1808, the United States government tried to stop the crossings by making it illegal to bring slaves into the country. The law did not stop people from buying and selling slaves who were already here, however. And **smugglers** still brought slaves over from Africa illegally, although the new law did reduce the number.

SLAVES COULD BE PUNISHED SEVERELY FOR ALMOST ANYTHING—INCLUDING NOT WORKING HARD ENOUGH OR TRYING TO ESCAPE. MANY, LIKE THE MAN SHOWN ABOVE, HAD TERRIBLE SCARS AFTER SUFFERING YEARS OF CRUEL PUNISHMENT.

Resistance

During the time of slavery, many whites lived in fear that their slaves would rebel or fight back. Their fears were well founded. Newspapers regularly reported instances of slaves poisoning or stabbing their owners. Other slaves harmed themselves as a way of fighting back. Some shot themselves in the hand or foot so they could not work for their masters. Others killed themselves to end a lifetime of slavery. Thousands of enslaved Africans ran away. These runaways cost their owners a great deal of money.

Other slaves organized groups of slaves to rise up against their masters. The greatest example of such a revolt took place not in the United States but in Haiti, on the island of Hispaniola. In the 1790s, Toussaint L'Ouverture (pronounced too-SAYN loo-ver-TOOR) led thousands of slaves in an uprising against French slave owners. The slaves defeated the French army, drove the French off the island, and won their independence.

In the United States, Gabriel Prosser led a famous attempted revolt in 1800. More than one thousand Virginia blacks, headed by Prosser, armed themselves and marched on Richmond, Virginia. The revolt fell apart at the last minute after two slaves reported the plan to whites. The governor of Virginia sent troops to crush the uprising. Prosser and the other leaders were captured and executed.

Denmark Vessey led a similar attempt in Charlestown, South Carolina. In 1822, Vessey was a free black. He had bought his own freedom more than 20 years earlier. For many years, Vessey gathered weapons and helpers with the aim of overthrowing slavery in the region. Some people estimate that more than 9,000 slaves were involved in the plot. With so many people involved, it is not surprising that word reached the government.

ONE SUCCESSFUL SLAVE REBELLION OCCURRED ON THE ISLAND OF HISPANIOLA. LED BY TOUSSAINT L'OUVERTURE, THOUSANDS OF SLAVES FOUGHT FOR INDEPENDENCE AGAINST WHITE LANDOWNERS.

Before Vessey's revolt could begin, 139 blacks were arrested. Forty-seven of them were executed. Four whites also went to prison for helping with the revolt.

A slave and preacher named Nat Turner led the most successful slave revolt in the United States. In 1831, Turner and a group of other blacks killed about 60 whites in Southampton, Virginia. State and federal troops eventually stopped Turner's small army. Turner escaped but was later captured and executed. Turner's revolt encouraged many blacks to fight for their freedom. It also horrified many whites because it destroyed their belief that blacks were happy to be enslaved.

Many enslaved blacks freed themselves. Every year, thousands of slaves ran to freedom. Some escaped alone, but many others had help from the **Underground Railroad.** The Underground Railroad was not an actual railroad. Instead, it was a group of black and white people in both the North and the South who helped blacks escape slavery. These helpers gave the runaways food and shelter during the long journey north. Some "conductors" on the Underground Railroad went with the runaways, directing them to safety. The most famous conductor was Harriet Tubman. She escaped slavery herself as a young woman but returned to the South many times to help other slaves escape.

Library of Congress

NOT ALL PEOPLE WHO FOUGHT SLAVERY WERE BLACK. JOHN BROWN, SHOWN ABOVE, WAS A FIERCE ABOLITIONIST WHO FOUGHT THE SPREAD OF SLAVERY TO NEW TERRITORIES.

Escaping slavery was not easy. The runaways had to travel hundreds of miles on foot. They moved by night and hid during the day. They often disguised themselves to avoid capture. They had to avoid dogs that could track them by scent. Most important, they had to avoid **patrols** and **bounty hunters.** Patrols were groups of armed whites who regularly traveled an area, looking for runaway blacks. Bounty hunters chased and caught runaways to collect a reward or "bounty" for their return. A slave was worth a great deal of money. Often slave owners hired bounty hunters to help recover their missing "property."

AFTER ESCAPING SLAVERY, HARRIET TUBMAN WENT BACK TO THE SOUTH 19 TIMES TO HELP OTHER SLAVES ESCAPE. SHE IS SHOWN BELOW (AT FAR LEFT) WITH SOME OF THOSE SHE HELPED.

Corbis/Bettmann

Slavery's End

By the 1830s, enslaved blacks had become one of the largest work forces on Earth. In many parts of the South, black slaves far outnumbered white people. But many people were questioning the practice of slavery. How could a nation founded on "life, liberty and the pursuit of happiness" deny even the most basic freedoms to millions of human beings? As slavery grew, so did **opposition** to it.

Northerners, both black and white, spoke out more and more against slavery. People who opposed slavery called themselves "abolitionists" because they wanted to abolish or end slavery. Many of these abolitionists wanted to see slavery end right away. Several antislavery newspapers sprang up in the North. The most famous was called the *Liberator.* It appeared in January of 1831. The editor, a white man named William Lloyd Garrison, became one of the nation's most outspoken critics of slavery.

Two years before the *Liberator* appeared, a free black man named David Walker printed a powerful essay. In it he declared that black people had the right to resist slavery—with force, if necessary. His powerful words terrified many whites. They also challenged blacks to win their freedom. Dozens of abolitionists formed groups, wrote letters to the government, and gave lectures condemning slavery. Abolitionists helped slaves escape through the Underground Railroad. Many women took a special interest in abolishing slavery. Women like Sojourner Truth, Lucretia Mott, and Lydia Marie Child all believed that a nation that enslaved blacks would never fully respect the rights of women.

Perhaps the greatest of all the abolitionists was Frederick Douglass. Douglass learned to read while enslaved in the South. He escaped slavery as a young man and became the nation's most forceful antislavery speaker and writer.

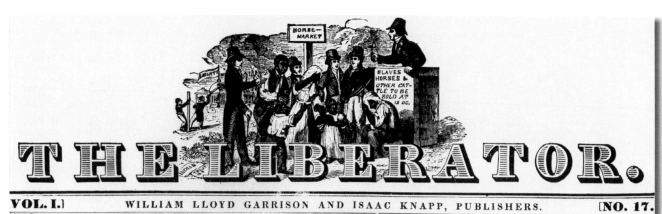

THE LIBERATOR.

VOL. I.]　WILLIAM LLOYD GARRISON AND ISAAC KNAPP, PUBLISHERS.　**[NO. 17.**

BOSTON, MASSACHUSETTS.]　OUR COUNTRY IS THE WORLD—OUR COUNTRYMEN ARE MANKIND.　[SATURDAY, APRIL 23, 1831.

THE LIBERATOR
IS PUBLISHED WEEKLY
AT NO. 11, MERCHANTS' HALL.

WM. LLOYD GARRISON, EDITOR.

TERMS.

☞ Two Dollars per annum, payable in advance.
☞ Agents allowed every sixth copy.
☞ No subscription will be received for a shorter period than six months.
☞ All letters and communications must be POST PAID.

AGENTS.
CHARLES WHIPPLE, *Newburyport, Mass.*
JAMES E. ELLIS, *Providence, R. I.*
PHILIP A. BELL, *New-York City.*
JOSEPH CASSEY, *Philadelphia, Pa.*
HENRY OGDEN, *Newark, N. J.*
WILLIAM WATKINS, *Baltimore, Md.*

THE LIBERATOR.

' Is not the plea, that emancipation is impracticable, the most impudent hypocrisy and the most glaring absurdity ever propounded for contemplation ?—Can any suppositions expediency, any dread of political disorder, or any private advantage, justify the prolongation of corruption, the enormity of which is unequalled, or repel the holy claim to its extinction ? The system is so entirely corrupt, that it admits of no cure but by a TOTAL and IMMEDIATE abolition. For a gradual emancipation is a virtual recognition of the right, and establishes the rectitude of the practice. If it be just for one moment, it is hallowed for ever ; and it be inequitable, not a day should it be tolerated.'
BOURNE.

two committee men and a constable interfered, and would not permit him to take his seat ! He was finally driven away, and the pew passed into other hands.

We purpose shortly to visit all our meeting-houses, and ascertain what places are provided for the accommodation of our colored people. A house dedicated to the worship of Almighty God, should be the last place for the exercise of despotic principles.—But here is the extract :

' With deep regret we have observed some articles in the columns of the " Liberator," of Boston, apparently from this city, in which its inhabitants are implicated ; and which we believe the editor of that publication will deem very injudicious, as well as unkind, when knowing the truth in the case. So far from wishing to deprive the colored population of an opportunity to worship God, by the co-operation of the friends of religion with that part of the inhabitants, a good and convenient house was erected a few years since ; clergymen of different denominations have often officiated, gratuitously, from Sabbath to Sabbath ; and when disappointed in the labors of a Minister, lay brethren have attended at their request, and made exertions to promote the prosperity of their congregation ; for many years a Sabbath School has been taught, composed entirely of colored children and adults ; in addition to this, if we mistake not, at their request the public school money is given them in proportion to the number of their children, and they thus have a day school of their own.

After such interest had been shown for that class of people, was it to be expected that an attack should be made upon the very persons who have shown such liberality ? This is indeed gratifying to the enemies of benevolent exertions : and were the

be elevated and improved in this country ; unanimous in opposing their instruction ; unanimous in exciting the prejudices of the people against them ; unanimous in apologising for the crime of slavery ; unanimous in conceding the right of the planters to hold their slaves in a limited bondage ; unanimous in denying the expediency of emancipation, unless the liberated slaves are sent to Liberia ; unanimous in their hollow pretence for colonizing, namely, to evangelize Africa ; unanimous in their *true motive* for the measure—a terror lest the blacks should rise to avenge their accumulated wrongs. It is a conspiracy to send the free people of color to Africa under a benevolent pretence, but really that the slaves may be held more securely in bondage.' It is a conspiracy based upon fear, oppression and falsehood, which draws its aliment from the prejudices of the people, which is sustained by duplicity, which is impotent in its design, which really upholds the slave system, which fascinates while it destroys, which endangers the safety and happiness of the country, which no precept of the bible can justify, which is implacable in its spirit, which should be annihilated at a blow.

These are our accusations ; and if we do not substantiate them, we are willing to be covered with reproach.

In attacking the principles, and exposing the evil tendency of the Society, we wish no one to understand us as saying, that all its friends are equally guilty, or actuated by the same motives. Nor let him suppose, that we exonerate any of them from reprehension. In various parts of the country there

virtue. I doubt not this conviction will ultimately prevail in every community, where the obligations of religion and philanthropy are acknowledged ; though the process may be slow ; having to contend with much ignorance prejudice and error. This conviction, however, is but the first step towards a result so desirable as the total abolition of slavery. Every long established custom acquires a strong hold on the feelings of those who are habituated to its control ; we know that its power in many cases is almost unconquerable ; and this is especially the case, where a custom, however injurious in its tendencies, is a source of pecuniary emolument, or worldly aggrandizement to those interested in its continuance. It therefore becomes necessary for the attainment of this great and good object—the universal emancipation of our colored brethren the complete overthrow of this abominable traffic in human flesh—to investigate the whole subject fairly and calmly ; to discuss it fully and freely ; to ascertain, as far as possible, what are the best means and methods for the accomplishment of this great end. On this point, I find there is great diversity of opinion. Men of equal talents, equal piety, and equal benevolence, take different and almost opposite views of the whole subject : my mind has been much perplexed, by hearing what seemed to me very strong arguments on both sides of the question.

With regard to the main subject, universal emancipation, as I before remarked, I have no doubt. I think it may, and it ought to be accomplished ; but with regard to the means of its accomplishment, I do not feel so decided. I wish

AS MORE PEOPLE BEGAN TO OPPOSE SLAVERY, BOOKS AND NEWSPAPERS WERE PUBLISHED TO SPEAK OUT AGAINST IT. THE *LIBERATOR* WAS ONE NEWSPAPER DEDICATED TO THE ABOLITIONIST CAUSE.

Library of Congress

Douglass eventually created his own antislavery newspaper called the *North Star*. He chose the name because runaway slaves often used the North Star to guide them at night. In 1845, Douglass published his own story, called *Narrative of the Life of Frederick Douglass, An American Slave*. The book became a best-seller and is now considered an American classic.

Douglass and the other abolitionists convinced many Northerners to oppose slavery. They helped shape widespread opinions against slavery. As antislavery beliefs grew, the nation became more and more divided.

In the mid-1800s, the United States of America was still expanding. American troops battled Native Americans and Mexico for control of land west of the Mississippi River. Each time the United States took more land, the big question was, Is this land free territory or slave territory? Most Southerners wanted slavery in the new territories. Most Northerners did not. Disagreement in the territories became so strong that settlers who had come from the North and South began to fight each other.

Disagreement was serious in the United States Congress as well. Representatives and senators from the South threatened to withdraw their states from the **Union** if they were not allowed to bring slavery into the new territories. They believed that individual states should be able to decide this issue. Northerners believed the national government should decide. The United States faced a major crisis. If Southern states left the Union, or **seceded,** the government would have to use force to bring them back.

The disagreement helped drive the United States toward a civil war, with the North and South ready to fight each other. After Abraham Lincoln was elected president in 1860, several Southern states decided to secede and form their own country. The Southerners believed that Lincoln was an abolitionist who wanted to destroy slavery. When Southern troops attacked a U.S. fort on April 12, 1861, Union troops fought back. The Civil War had begun.

At the start of the war, slavery was not the main issue. President Lincoln knew that many Northerners would not fight a war to free slaves, but they would fight to preserve the Union. Southerners said they were fighting for individual states' rights. Even so, black people knew that the war could decide the future of slavery. They volunteered by the thousands to fight for the North.

At first, the Union army turned away black volunteers. Even though many Northerners opposed slavery, they still had racist beliefs. But after Union troops lost battle after battle to the South, the North decided to allow blacks to join the Union Army. Blacks knew that this was their time to fight for freedom. Thousands of free blacks joined the army, and thousands more escaped slavery to join as well.

Black troops were not treated as equals. They received lower pay and poor equipment. At first, they were not even allowed to fight in battles. But the South kept beating the North in battle, and the Union Army needed more troops. Eventually, the Union Army treated its black troops better.

Although the Civil War was fought for a number of reasons, it did finally lead to the end of slavery. In January of 1863, President Lincoln issued the Emancipation Proclamation, which freed slaves in all the rebel states. Lincoln did not have the power to enforce the proclamation at that time. But the act itself helped the North in its fight.

Black troops fought bravely in many battles, helping the North win the Civil War. They fought to keep the nation together, but they also fought for freedom—for themselves and for others. People knew that if the South won the war, slavery would continue for a long time. When the North won in 1865, the end of slavery was finally in sight.

Slavery did not end right away, however. The United States had to pass **amendments** to the Constitution to put an end to slavery for good. The 13th Amendment made slavery illegal. The 14th Amendment said that all former slaves were citizens, like anyone else born in the United States.

The 15th Amendment gave African American men the right to vote. (Women of all races could not vote in the United States until 1920.)

The end of slavery did not mean the end of racism. The government did not always enforce these new amendments to the Constitution. The end of slavery was just the beginning of another long journey—the struggle to bring equal treatment to all people. That journey continues even today.

To commit to equality means being free of all racism. Slavery was a terrible institution that destroyed the lives of many people. Nonetheless, the survival and resistance of millions of enslaved blacks pointed this nation toward a truer freedom and a more genuine equality.

Library of Congress

SLAVERY ENDED IN 1865, BUT LIFE DID NOT CHANGE VERY MUCH FOR MOST
AFRICAN AMERICANS. MANY, LIKE THE FARM WORKERS SHOWN ABOVE, STILL
WORKED ON THE PLANTATIONS WHERE THEY HAD BEEN HELD AS SLAVES. OTHERS
COULD FIND NO WORK AND HAD DIFFICULTY SUPPORTING THEMSELVES AND THEIR
FAMILIES. NONE WERE TREATED AS EQUAL CITIZENS OF THE UNITED STATES.

Timeline

1501	Europeans begin transporting enslaved Africans to the Western Hemisphere to replace Native American slaves.
1619	The first enslaved Africans land in North America at the settlement of Jamestown, Virginia. All 13 colonies will participate in slavery.
1776	The United States declares its independence from England. Thomas Jefferson writes in the Declaration of Independence that "all men are created equal."
1787	The Constitution of the United States allows slavery to exist in the new nation.
1800	Gabriel Prosser leads a large but unsuccessful slave revolt in Virginia.
1808	A new law makes it illegal to bring slaves to the United States from Africa.
1822	Denmark Vessey, a free black man, plots a large slave revolt in South Carolina. Whites discover the plot, and the revolt never takes place.
1831	A white abolitionist named William Lloyd Garrison founds an antislavery newspaper called the *Liberator*.
	Nat Turner leads a Virginia slave rebellion in which about 60 whites are killed. Turner and his men are eventually captured and executed.
1847	Frederick Douglass, a black abolitionist and fugitive slave, starts an antislavery newspaper called the *North Star*.
1860	Abraham Lincoln is elected president of the United States. Southerners are furious because they believe he is an abolitionist who will end slavery.
1861	Many Southern states leave the United States because they want the right to expand slavery into the new territories. This action leads to the Civil War, which begins on April 12.
1863	Abraham Lincoln issues the Emancipation Proclamation.
1865	The North defeats the South in the Civil War. The 13th Amendment to the U.S. Constitution declares slavery to be illegal.
1868	The 14th Amendment to the Constitution grants full citizenship to all former slaves.
1870	The 15th Amendment guarantees African American men the right to vote.

Glossary

abolished (uh-BOL-ishd)
When something is abolished, it is officially ended. In the United States, slavery was finally abolished after the end of the Civil War.

abolitionist (ab-uh-LIH-shun-ist)
An abolitionist was a person who wanted to end slavery. Frederick Douglass was a famous abolitionist.

amendments (uh-MEND-ments)
Amendments are changes made to a law or an official document. Amendments to the United States Constitution ended slavery.

bondage (BON-dedj)
People who are kept in bondage are held against their will. Enslaved Africans were held in bondage.

bounty hunters (BOWN-tee HUN-terz)
Bounty hunters are people who are rewarded for catching fugitives. Bounty hunters tracked and captured escaped slaves.

Civil War (SIV-il WAR)
A civil war is a war fought between different groups within the same country. The U.S. Civil War was fought between the North and the South from 1861 to 1865.

clans (KLANZ)
Clans are groups of related families. African tribes and clans often had very different religious traditions and customs.

Constitution (kon-stih-TOO-shun)
A constitution is a document that lays out how a nation's government and laws will work. The U.S. Constitution was written more than 200 years ago.

dependent (dee-PEN-dent)
If people are dependent, they rely on others for help or support. Slave masters wanted their slaves to be completely dependent on them.

diverse (dih-VERS)
Something that is diverse is made up of very different things. The continent of Africa has a diverse population.

enslaved (en-SLAYVD)
When people are enslaved, they are forced to be slaves or are owned by other people. Millions of enslaved Africans were brought to North and South America.

fugitive (FYOO-jih-tiv)
A fugitive is a person who is running away from someone or something, especially from the law. Runaway slaves were fugitives, with slave owners and others trying to hunt them down.

Glossary

inhumane (in-hyoo-MAYN)
Something that is inhumane is unkind or cruel.
Slaves were often treated inhumanely.

opposition (op-eh-ZISH-un)
Opposition is action against something. As
slavery spread in the United States, opposition
to it grew stronger.

overseer (OH-vur-see-ur)
An overseer is a person who supervises others
as they work. Plantation owners hired overseers
to supervise slaves.

patrols (puh-TROLZ)
Patrols are groups of people who make rounds
to guard or look for something. During the time
of slavery, patrols searched for fugitive slaves.

plantations (plan-TAY-shunz)
Plantations are large farms that grow warm-
weather crops such as cotton, rubber, and
coffee. Years ago, slaves were often forced to
work on plantations.

prejudice (PREH-juh-diss)
Prejudice is an unfair opinion or judgment about
someone or something. Even after slavery ended,
prejudices about race continued.

profit (PROF-it)
In business, profit is money that is left over
after all expenses are paid. Slave traders often
made a large profit.

racism (RAY-siz-um)
Racism is a belief that people of one color or race
are better than people of another race. Racism
remained a problem even after slavery ended.

seceded (sih-SEED-ed)
A group member that has seceded has left the
group against the wishes of other members.
During the Civil War, Southern states seceded
from the United States and formed their
own country.

smugglers (SMUG-glerz)
Smugglers bring goods into a place illegally.
Bringing slaves into the United States became
illegal, but smugglers still brought them in.

**Underground Railroad
(UN-der-grownd RAYL-rohd)**
The Underground Railroad was a network of
people in the North and South who helped
blacks escape slavery. Many people worked hard
to make the Underground Railroad a success.

Union (YOON-yen)
The Union is another name for the United
States. During the Civil War, the term "Union"
referred to the Northern states.

Index

abolitionists, 19, 20, 28, 30-32, 33
Africa, 6, 8, 9, 10, 12, 14, 25
    culture of, 8, 10
    empires of, 8, 10
    languages of, 8
    people of, 6, 7, 8, 9, 10
    slavery in, 8, 10, 11
Arabia, 6

bounty hunters, 29
Brown, John, 28

Cape of Good Hope, 8
Caribbean Islands, 12
Central America, 12
Child, Lydia Marie, 30
China, 10
Civil War, 19, 33-34, 36
Columbus, Christopher, 36
Congress, U.S., 33
Constitution, U.S., 19, 34, 36
Cuba, 12

Declaration of Independence, 16, 36
Dominican Republic, 12, 36
Douglass, Frederick, 20, 22, 30, 36

Emancipation Proclamation, 34, 36
England, 16, 19
Europe, 6, 8, 10
European explorers, 10, 12, 36

15th Amendment, 34, 36
14th Amendment, 34, 36
"free blacks," 16, 19, 26, 30, 33
freedom, 8, 16, 17, 19, 30, 34
French slave owners, 26

Garrison, William Lloyd, 30, 36
Ghana, 10

Haiti, 12, 36
Hispaniola, 12, 26, 27, 36

India, 6, 10

Jamaica, 12
Jefferson, Thomas, 16, 17, 36

Kalahari desert, 8

the *Liberator,* 30, 31, 36
Lincoln, Abraham, 32, 33-34, 36
L'Ouverture, Toussaint, 26, 27

Mali, 10
Mediterranean Sea, 8
Mexico, 32
"Middle Passage," 14, 15
Mississippi, 32
Mott, Lucretia, 30

Narrative of the Life of Frederick Douglass, 32
Native Americans, 12, 32, 36
"New World," 6, 12, 14, 20. *See also* North America, South America
New York colony, 18
Nile River, 8
North Africa, 6
North America, 8, 10, 12, 13, 14, 16
the *North Star,* 32, 36
Northern states (the North), 18, 19, 30, 32-33

Old World. *See* Europe

plantations, 16, 19
Portugal, 6
prejudice, 6. *See also* racism
Prosser, Gabriel, 26, 36
Puerto Rico, 12

racism, 6, 33, 34
Richmond, Virginia, 26

Sahara desert, 8
slave quarters, 22, 24
slavery
    in Africa, 8, 10, 11
    in Europe, 8, 10
    history of, 6, 7, 8
    laws on, 8, 10, 16, 24, 36
    in North America, 8, 10, 13
    opposition to, 30, 31. *See also* abolitionists
    punishment of, 20, 25
slaves
    auction of, 20, 21
    citizenship of, 34, 35
    education of, 22
    rebellion and escape of, 26-29, 30, 32
    rights of, 25
    treatment of, 6, 10, 14, 20, 22-25
slave ships, 6, 8, 14, 15, 16
slave trade, 6, 7, 8, 11, 12, 14, 36
    in Africa, 10, 11
Songhay, 10
South America, 10, 12
South Carolina, 36
Southern states (the South), 16, 18, 19, 30, 32-33

13th Amendment, 34, 36
Truth, Sojourner, 30, 32
Tubman, Harriet, 28, 29
Turner, Nat, 28, 36

Underground Railroad, 28, 30
Union army, 33
United States, 6, 16, 17, 19, 28, 32, 34, 36

Walker, David, 30
Washington, George, 16, 17
West Africa, 6
women's rights, 30, 34

Further Information

Books and Magazines

Douglass, Frederick. *Narrative of the Life of Frederick Douglass.* New York: Penguin Books, 1986.

Kent, Deborah. *African Americans in the Thirteen Colonies* (Cornerstones of Freedom). New York: Childrens Press, 1996.

Lester, Julius. *To Be A Slave.* New York: Scholastic Inc., 1968.

Myers, Walter Dean. *Now Is Your Time: The African-American Struggle for Freedom.* New York: HarperCollins Children's Books, 1991.

Westridge Young Writer's Workshop. *Kid's Explore America's African American Heritage.* Santa Fe, NM: John Muir Publications, 1993.

Williams, Carla. *The Underground Railroad.* Chanhassen, MN: The Child's World, 2002.

Web Sites

See a more detailed timeline about the history of slavery:
http://innercity.org/holt/slavechron.html

View a catalog of slavery images:
http://lcweb.loc.gov/rr/print/082_slave.html

Learn more about slavery:
http://www.iron.k12.ut.us/schools.csm/resource/slav.html

Find links to numerous sites with information about slavery:
http://www.coax.net/people/LWF/slavery.htm

View the Library of Congress's Web site on slavery:
http://memory.loc.gov/ammem/aaohtml/exhibit/aopart1.html

View the Smithsonian Institution's Web site on slavery, including audio clips
of slave narratives:
http://rememberingslavery.org/